Leading With Empathy
in a
Remote Work World

Leading With Empathy in a Remote Work World

*Develop Connection
and
Improve Productivity
in the New Working Environment*

Melissa Harris

Table of Contents

Introduction

Welcome to the world of remote work, where you can hold business meetings in your pajamas, interact with colleagues from the comfort of your sofa, and skip that annoying morning drive. It is a world of ease and flexibility, but it's not without its drawbacks. The development of remote work has revolutionized how we work and affected how we lead.

In this new context, the concept of empathy in leadership is more vital than ever before. We must learn to negotiate the intricacies of remote work with a clear knowledge of our colleagues' needs, emotions, and viewpoints. We must be able to promote connection, develop trust, and inspire cooperation, even when we are miles apart.

So, what precisely is empathy, and why is it so vital in leading people successfully? How can we build and maintain it in a remote work environment? And most importantly, how can we use it to build a more productive, connected, and rewarding workplace for ourselves and our teams?

Before we take a deep dive and answer these questions, let's quickly examine the concept of empathy, its relevance to leadership, and challenges posed by a remote work setting.

Accessing empathy is an essential talent for a leader or manager, particularly in today's remote work environment. Without the advantage of face-to-face encounters, it may be difficult to judge the emotional condition of your team members. Misunderstandings may occur, which may cause hurtful reactions, or feelings of loneliness might sneak in. That's why understanding empathy is necessary and useful.

So, what exactly is empathy?

> *Empathy is the ability to understand and share in the feelings of others. It is the ability to walk a mile in someone else's shoes, to view things from their perspective, and to react with compassion and love.*

And when it comes to managing humans, a temperament of understanding and compassion can give any leader or manager an edge. It helps you to connect with your team on a deeper level, realize their problems and issues, and react with kindness and support.

It can be easier said than done in a typical office environment where everyone is physically present, so how can it work in a remote work situation when the team is not present? Not having the chance to see your team members in person can make it more difficult to notice nonverbal signs or interpret their moods, however you can learn the skills to do it!

As an effective leader, it is your obligation to seek to develop empathy in your leadership style deliberately. You must actively listen to your team members and take the time to gage their personalities and to understand their unique issues. It also involves establishing a culture of inclusion and cooperation where everyone feels heard and respected.

Creating empathy in a distance work setting requires conscious and focused effort. You may need to be creative with your communication techniques, employing video conferencing or instant messaging to maintain contact with your team members. Scheduling time for frequent check-ins when you can catch up on both work-related and personal concerns. And you may need to have patience, since it takes time to develop trust with your team members.

The advantages of empathetic leadership are clear. Your team members will feel more connected, more supported, and more inspired to produce their best work. And as a leader, you will be better positioned to direct them towards success. Therefore, embrace and incorporate empathy into your management style and watch your team develop.

This book is your practical guide to learning to lead with empathy in all settings, but particularly in a remote work setting. From understanding the science of empathy to building emotional intelligence to cultivating empathy in teams and overcoming hurdles, we will cover the various facets of this subtle but important leadership talent. Using real-world examples, practical recommendations and insightful counsel, you will discover that communicating effectively, managing from a place of compassion, and developing a culture of true connection is well worth the effort in your organization.

This book is also interactive. It is meant to be written in and highlighted. Questions at the end of each chapter are meant to challenge your thinking and help you evaluate your organization, your team, and your own leadership skills.

The tips found within these pages are applicable whether you are a new manager supervising a remote team or a seasoned remote work leader. Are you ready to uncover the power of empathy and learn how to apply it to improve the outcomes of your remote work team?

Chapter 1 Understanding Empathy

As leaders in our respective organizations, we are charged to focus on tasks, deadlines, and goals. The output of products and services is the driver of the company's bottom line. However, it takes qualified, knowledgeable, and motivated personnel to make that bottom line a reality. As the world advances and we find ourselves at the heart of a remote work environment, we must gain the essential trait that distinguishes us as good managers and binds our teams together for the common goal - empathy.

Empathy is not merely a soft characteristic but the backbone of leadership. It is the ability to put oneself in someone else's shoes, to grasp their thoughts, ideas, and emotions, and to react appropriately. It is not just about being nice or friendly but about generating relationships, and ultimately a work environment, where people feel listened to, respected, and valued.

As we have all heard – people are the greatest asset in any organization. Exhibiting empathy becomes an even more vital skill in remote work situations, where in-person meetings are limited. As managers, we must be in touch consistently with our team members' roles and challenges and provide support, guidance, and encouragement. We must also realize that our employees are not only their job titles but real people with families, lives, and expectations.

So how can we as leaders cultivate empathy? Is it something we are born with, or can it be learned? The good news is that empathy can be created and improved through practice.

In this chapter, we will cover the multiple qualities of empathy, including the science behind it, its benefits, and how to foster empathy in a remote work setting. We will give practical ideas and techniques for leaders to communicate with empathy, increase emotional intelligence, and cultivate understanding within their workforce.

> *Empathy is the capacity to comprehend and share the feelings of another person. It is a*

skill of placing oneself in someone else's shoes and experiencing the world through their eyes.

In the fast-paced and ever-changing world of business, empathy is a beneficial tool for leaders and managers alike. As a leader, you are responsible for steering your team toward success, and employing empathy can help you develop great connections with your team members. When you express this skill, you show your team members that you care about them as individuals, not simply as workers. You create an atmosphere where people feel appreciated, respected, and heard.

Let me share a tale to highlight the power of empathy. A few years ago, I managed a team of developers on a significant IT project. One of my team members, Sarah, was trying to keep up with the workload. I could see that she was worried and overloaded, and her work product was deteriorating.

Instead of urging Sarah to work more or pressuring her to meet deadlines, I adopted a more compassionate approach. I sat down with her and asked her how she was feeling. I listened to her worries and recognized her challenges. I told her I realized the assignment's challenge and appreciated her hard work.

Following our chat, Sarah appeared to have renewed enthusiasm and purpose. She felt heard and encouraged, and her work product started to improve. By taking the time to listen to Sarah and understand her viewpoint, I was able to create a closer connection with her and help her in creating a more effective process to complete her assignment.

To have moments like this, you must learn how to tap into the compassionate side of your personality. But how do you cultivate empathy as a leader?

First, you need to consciously <u>listen</u> to your team members. When someone comes to you with an issue or worry, genuinely hear them. Ask questions and indicate that you are interested in their thoughts and opinions.

Second, try to place yourself in their shoes. Consider what you would think and how you would feel if you were in their circumstances. Understanding their feelings and motives can lead to more successful communication and problem-solving.

Lastly, be <u>real</u> in your relationships with your team members. Authenticity is crucial when it comes to developing trust and rapport. People can sense when someone is not being sincere with them, or not telling them the "truth". As you display empathy, be sure it comes from a place of real concern and care.

Often, leaders or managers do not take the time to listen, understand, or even assist their team members. Many leaders do not understand the science underpinning empathy or how it can help them establish better connections, foster a more favorable workplace culture, and ultimately drive success for their organization.

The Science Behind Empathy

You may have heard the term empathy tossed about in various settings. But have you ever paused to study the science underlying empathy and why it can be so helpful in the workplace?

First, let us recall our definition of empathy. It can be described as the ability to comprehend and share the sentiments of others. Empathy is not sympathy. Leaders and managers often do not grasp that empathy goes beyond pity, which is merely feeling sorry for someone. Empathy is not a passive feeling, but an active one. It demands attentive listening, perspective-taking, and genuine care for others.

Now, let us investigate the science supporting empathy. The human brain is wired for empathetic responses. When we witness someone suffering pain or enjoying pleasure, parts of the brain light up as if we were experiencing those feelings ourselves. This is known as *neuronal resonance*. In other words, our brains have the power to mimic the emotions of others, enabling us to connect to them on a deeper level.

Yet empathy is not a reflexive reaction. It requires intention and practice. This is where *emotional regulation* comes into play. Emotional regulation is the capacity to govern our own emotions in reaction to the emotions of others. It helps us respond in a helpful and supportive manner rather than allowing ourselves to get entangled in our own emotions within the situation. It's the ability to set our feelings aside temporarily, so that we can truly attempt to connect to and understand the feelings of others.

Sharing empathy in the workplace develops feelings of belonging and connection among team members. We are all more willing to trust and work with others when we feel seen and heard. Empathy also allows us to perceive and react to the needs of others, whether it be offering help at a difficult time or recognizing and applauding a job well done.

Empathy empowers managers to realize the views of their employees, which in turn enables them to make better decisions that consider the interests and concerns of everyone involved. As a conscious process, building empathy includes *active listening* as a main component. Active listening involves setting aside your personal agenda and focusing on what the other person is saying. It is assessing tone of voice and reading body language to form a complete picture of the message. It is being truly open and interested, asking questions to understand their viewpoint and experience better.

Another important part of the process is *perspective-taking*. This implies setting oneself in someone else's shoes and trying to see their point of view. You may not agree with their viewpoint, but understanding where they are coming from can be invaluable to finding a common ground and resolving an issue.

Finally, *emotional management* is a key component for improving empathetic skills. Being aware of your own emotions and controlling them in a manner that enables you to react to others in a supportive and helpful way is key. Leaders who can regulate personal emotions find it easier to respond rationally under stress and take more effective action.

The Benefits of Empathy in Leadership

As we all know, success is not simply reaching goals, meeting deadlines, and making money. It's about developing a strong, motivated staff invested in the organization's long-term objectives. And believe it or not, one of the most effective weapons in your arsenal is empathy. When you lead with empathy, you can connect with your team on a deeper level, develop trust, and create an atmosphere where people feel respected and supported, which in turn promotes loyalty and staff retention.

There are proven advantages of incorporating empathy in your leadership style.

Better communication

When you take the time to actively listen to your team members and be open to their viewpoints, communication is more effective. Employing empathy allows you to detect the emotions underlying the words that someone is speaking, which may help you to react more positively and to prevent misunderstandings.

As an example, I was managing a team that was struggling with a challenging project. One team member, John, appeared unusually agitated during a team meeting. Instead of merely asking John to "buckle down" and finish the task so we could make the deadline, I chose a more compassionate approach. I decided to speak with John individually to find the source of his agitation. I listened to his worries and did my best to understand his viewpoint. He shared some valuable information, and I was able to address the underlying problem and develop a solution that helped not only him but also the rest of the team. I saw John become more enthused with his part of the project and his performance improved. Collectively, the team functioned better, and further tension was minimized.

Improved buy-in and motivation

When employees feel that their leaders care about them as individuals, they are more likely to be engaged and driven. Empathy enables you to connect with your team members on a human level, which can build feelings of loyalty and dedication. Consider, for instance, the example of John. After listening to John, we developed an improved strategy, and his desire to do a good job on the project was strengthened.

I once had a team member battling a personal problem outside of work that was affecting her concentration and attention at work. Instead of simply addressing only her work product, I took the time to check in with her on a personal level and ask about her situation. She felt encouraged and supported, not only on a professional level but a personal level too. And thus, our relationship was enhanced. She began to see me as a supervisor who cared, which invoked a sense of loyalty toward the team. We must recognize that personal lives and working lives are intertwined, and one will affect the other.

Greater ties and trust

Better connections with your team members are realized when you lead with empathy. Developing a culture of trust and cooperation can promote greater teamwork and, eventually, better outcomes.

I was leading a team through a large organizational shift. We were outsourcing some of the operations and re-organizing the teams that remained. This was a difficult period for everyone, as individuals were anxious about job security and the organization's future. Instead of merely concentrating on the tasks at hand, I set aside time to personally engage with each team member, listening to their worries, answering questions, and supplying encouragement. This helped develop trust and generated a feeling of togetherness within the team – that we were all in it together – allowing us to navigate the transformation effectively.

Significant change is often necessary in an organization but can be one of the scariest occurrences in the workplace, particularly when it concerns job security. Confusion and panic among the team members often abounds and lowered productivity occurs due to those feelings. By sharing information consistently, such as the next steps, the timeline, and the daily progress with the members, along with an uplifted attitude and encouraging words, a leader can make a difficult process more calming and ultimately successful.

Promoting creativity and innovation

When individuals feel comfortable expressing their thoughts and viewpoints, they are more likely to develop inventive solutions to challenges. Empathy helps to establish an atmosphere where individuals feel secure to express themselves, which may lead to more creative and effective problem-solving.

During an interview with Evan, a potential new employee, he professed quite a remarkable record and success at his former place of employment. I hired Evan. But after starting work in my team, Evan did not fulfill the lofty expectations I had for him. If you have been in this situation before, you will understand the disappointment that comes with it.

Evan was unusually quiet and restrained at meetings and didn't contribute much. Through active observation and picturing myself in Evan's place as a new employee, I discovered that Evan was intimidated by some of the more vocal team members. For me, this was a big breakthrough. I altered our meeting agendas and facilitation practices in a manner that created a safer space for Evan to contribute. We were then able to tap into his imagination and produce some incredibly unique solutions. In a more collaborative environment, he had a lot to share!

Better employee retention

When individuals feel appreciated and supported at work, they are more likely to remain with the organization long-term. Solidifying empathy within a workplace culture helps establish a feeling of belonging and loyalty, which may increase employee retention.

Understanding empathy and how to apply it is a tool for every leader and manager's toolbox. It helps to enhance communication, promote engagement and motivation, form trust and relationships, stimulate creativity and innovation, and improve employee retention rates. Leading with empathy can build a strong and cohesive team that is aligned with the organization's objectives. Yet, as the leader, you must walk the walk and talk the talk.

1. What type of leader am I?

_____

_____

_____

_____

2. Do I understand empathy? How have I exercised it recently? Identify an example.

_____

_____

_____

_____

3. Reflect on each team member, or the group as a whole. Are they motivated? Is there trust?

_____

_____

_____

_____

4. List a few areas within the team that may need improvement.

_____

_____

_____

_____

Chapter 2 Building Empathy in a Remote Work Setting

The world of work has experienced a fundamental upheaval, with the barriers between work and life dissolving and physical offices giving way to virtual ones. The remote work environment is a new standard, and this "new normal" way of doing business requires empathy more than ever.

Yet, let's face it, managing employees, pursuing productivity, and identifying and resolving challenges in a remote work setting is no walk in the park. Creating relationships and building trust can be tough when you are not in the same physical area as your coworkers. So how can we establish a culture of empathy in this new world of work?

In this chapter, we'll dissect remote work issues and investigate approaches for promoting connection and empathy in a virtual context. We'll look at ways to develop a culture that supports inclusiveness, trust, and cooperation. We'll provide useful tactics for clarifying communication, active listening, and drawing team members together. Whether you are a leader, a manager, or a team member, you can learn to handle the hurdles of remote work, cultivate team connection, and establish meaningful relationships with individuals in a virtual setting.

Understanding the difficulties of remote work

As demand for remote work continues to grow, this employment perk also comes with its own set of obstacles. The following are four prevalent potential downsides to remote employment, from the perspective of the remote worker, along with example scenarios and outlined solutions.

Challenge #1: Isolation

Working from home may save time on long commutes or dollars spent on business wardrobes, however, it can be <u>isolating</u>. It may be difficult to keep motivated and interested when social connections, as you would have at an office, are lacking.

<u>The Isolation Trap</u>:

Mark was pleased to start his new remote job, but he soon found that working alone from his apartment was not as simple as he expected. He missed the companionship of the workplace and found it difficult to concentrate on his work tasks without the framework of a conventional workweek. He tried working from coffee shops but found them loud and distracting. Mark ultimately located a co-working location that enabled him to work among other remote workers and freelancers. He felt that having other people around helped him overcome the isolated feelings that were hindering his work progress.

Solution: Fight isolation by finding a community of remote workers, whether it's via a co-working facility or online forums, to integrate some social interaction into your day. There also may be opportunities to work in the office among your co-workers once or twice a week – a modified remote work schedule.

Challenge #2: Distractions

Although working from home can have many benefits, it can also be a breeding ground for distractions. Whether it is your dogs, your children, or your Netflix account, interruptions might make it tough to focus on work.

The Distraction Dilemma:

Jenny had always dreamed of working from home, but she didn't expect the disruptions that would come with it. Her kids, the dog, and social media accounts frequently interrupted her. Jenny attempted to create boundaries with her family but found it difficult to keep them. She finally devised and posted a time management plan that enabled her to work more effectively throughout the day, with break times identified to respond to her family and other commitments.

Solution: Limit interruptions and distractions by having an organized dedicated workspace, setting work versus personal time boundaries with family and friends, and adhering to a time management plan that works for your lifestyle.

Challenge #3: Time Management

Independently managing your time is as much a science as it is an art. Without the framework of a regular work schedule, it's easy to lose track of time and become less productive.

Time Management Trickiness:

David enjoyed the freedom of working remotely, but he battled managing his time properly. Without the framework of a typical 9 to 5 job in an office, he found himself working weird hours and losing track of time. David devised and documented a routine, including setting his preferred work hours during the day, along with a lunch period and breaks. He said "no" to accepting calls or performing tasks after his workday ended. He applied his new schedule consistently every day until it became a habit. He became more productive and organized through the process.

Solution: Manage your time efficiently by creating a work schedule, sticking to it, and using productivity tools to keep on track.

Challenge #4: Technology

Although technology has made remote work practical, it can also be a source of irritation. Bad internet connections, video conferencing software issues, and other technological challenges may create delays and reduce productivity.

Technology Troubles:

Initially, Tom had a tough time with technology when he began working remotely. He regularly had a terrible internet connection and struggled with video conferencing software that would freeze or crash. Tom finally researched and invested in an enhanced internet connectivity plan and discovered a more dependable video conferencing application, which resolved most of his daily tech challenges.

Solution: Address technological difficulties immediately by investing in dependable equipment, connections, and software. Your employer may require use of specific products or services and can assist if issues with them arise.

Techniques for Developing Empathy within a Remote Work Team

Introducing and establishing a long-term culture of empathy in a remote work setting takes planning, consistency, and patience. As a manager of a remote team, you may recognize disconnection, lack of communication, misunderstandings, and mistrust between your team members. This can lead to a team's poor performance and diminished productivity, which impacts the bottom line of the organization. As a manager, performing an unbiased assessment of your team is crucial to determine the strengths and weaknesses of your group's interactions. Collect information by measuring both group dynamics and individual competencies. Once you have completed a root-cause analysis of this information, you can then begin to apply the following strategies to the highest priority areas of lack on your team.

Arrange regular one-on-one meetings

Leaders and managers of remote workers are re-learning that it is critical to have regular one-on-one sessions with each team member. Utilize this opportunity to check their well-being and listen to any concerns. Be sure you provide them with your complete attention and actively listen to what they are saying. If not in person, then a video conference call should be used, so you can see each other. This opens communication channels and builds trust. This is also the time for coaching and addressing improvements in their work products and interactions with others if needed.

Promote open communication

Urge your team members to talk freely and honestly with you. Speak and act in a way that clearly displays that their thoughts and suggestions are welcome and will be treated with respect. By establishing a secure setting for free discussion, increased trust and confidence will develop.

Employ video conferencing

Video conferencing is a valuable tool for a distant work setting. Whether during a one-on-one or a full team meeting, observing your team members' expressions and body language will help you understand their message and their underlying feelings behind their words. You can also consider the interactions between team members more directly and identify potential disagreements or problems before they flourish. Requiring regular video conferencing within a team also reinforces your belief as the leader or manager in the importance of eye-to-eye interactions to your team, of which more personal connections can result.

Present virtual team-building activities

Developing empathy and connection between coworkers is not only about work-related encounters. Initiating opportunities for virtual team-building events may help your team members connect on a personal level with you and with each other. For example, you may plan a virtual game night once a week or a virtual coffee break once per day. There are many resources online to aid in brainstorming ideas. Organizations have instituted some creative ideas and are reaping the benefits of them!

Utilize in-person meetings as often as necessary

Even though workers may be remote and not in the office every day, you can still require that staffers make the commute to take part in an in-person individual or group meeting. Of course, identifying the most appropriate reasons and timing for this takes pre-planning and advance notification. An in-person team-building activity may also be a useful and fun part of this meeting. You may be surprised to learn that employees welcome the chance to come into the office and engage with their coworkers!

Demonstrate empathy towards your staff

A seasoned leader knows that leading by example is necessary to win the hearts and minds of the followers. Demonstrate empathy towards your team members by being accessible, understanding, and helpful. Take the time to get to know them personally, listen enthusiastically, and acknowledge their questions, issues, and situations.

Initiating and growing an empathetic environment in a remote work setting takes time and effort, but it is worth it. Building this type of culture will enhance communication, increase productivity, and promote morale. The integration of these strategies over time will dramatically improve your ability to establish a positive and supportive culture within your remote workforce.

Creating a Long-Term Culture of Empathy

The leader's involvement and initiative in fostering a healthy workplace culture cannot be understated. It is critical and the only way to make real lasting changes within the team. The manager sets the tone and promotes expectations and acceptable behavior of the team and its members. Clear fair rules, enforcement consistency, and accountability are a few elements that develop a positive culture over time. And it does take time. Here are more practical suggestions for fostering a long-term culture of empathy in your workplace.

Lead by Example

As a leader, your actions speak louder than words. To develop a culture of empathy, you must model compassionate conduct towards others yourself. Your staff need to see you setting the standard and modeling the behaviors you are requiring of them - listening, relating, encouraging, and reacting with transparency and compassion.

Promote Active Listening

Active listening is a critical component of empathy. Encourage your staff to listen closely to one another and to reply with respect and understanding. Provide training sessions and coaching in the area of active listening. It is a learned skill. There are many resources online to help identify training opportunities and courses.

Build Trust

Trust is vital in any work team. Empathy is based on trust – you cannot have one without the other. Build trust by being honest and straightforward with your staff in every situation, acknowledging your own errors, and supporting your team in their accomplishments as well as their failings.

Generate Occasions for Cooperation

Collaboration allows workers to engage together and comprehend one another's viewpoints while working toward a shared outcome. Promote cooperation by assigning team projects and offering opportunities for cross-functional teams to work together.

Celebrate Diversity

Accepting diversity is another pillar of fostering connection in the workplace. Acknowledge and appreciate your workers' varied backgrounds, experiences, and viewpoints. Build a safe and inclusive atmosphere where everyone feels valued and respected.

Offer Opportunities for Growth

A positive integrated culture includes urging your staff to continue to grow and develop personally and professionally. Promote professional growth, provide personal mentoring and coaching, and recognize and reward performance.

Advocate Open Communication

Open communication is the backbone of creating and sustaining an empathetic team culture. Encourage your staff to talk freely, respectfully, and honestly with one another. Identify and endorse proper outlets for constructive criticisms, suggestions and recommendations that can benefit the whole team.

Sustaining a long-term culture of empathy is a constant daily practice. It requires regular impartial assessments to understand what is working and what may not be, and adaptability to change practices and processes to create continuous improvements. By modeling empathetic behavior, encouraging active listening, building trust, promoting collaboration, celebrating diversity, supplying growth opportunities, and fostering open communication, you can create a workplace culture that values empathy and enhances employee satisfaction, productivity, and team performance.

Take a few moments to ask these questions and make notes of the answers. This simple assessment can then be the platform to identify where your team is and where you want it to be in terms of the principles of this book.

1. Have I noticed if staff may be having difficulties with working remotely? Who? How?

_____

_____

_____

_____

2. What is the true culture of my organization, and more specifically, my team?

_____

_____

_____

_____

3. What areas within the team are current problems, or may have been problems in the past?

_____

_____

_____

_____

4. Which techniques from this chapter could I begin to demonstrate and promote to help my team?

_____

_____

_____

_____

Chapter 3 Communicating with Empathy

Communication can make or break the success of any company or organization. As a leader or manager, not only must you speak, act, and respond appropriately, you must ensure that your team communicates effectively and efficiently also. Nonetheless, articulate communication extends beyond just sending and receiving spoken messages. Elements of listening, processing, observing, understanding, and responding also play important roles.

In this chapter, we will examine the skill of compassionate communication. Active listening, verbal, and non-verbal cues, and preventing misconceptions are just some of the subjects in this central topic.

As a leader, acquiring these abilities is crucial to develop strong connections with your team and to promote an open work environment.

Skill #1 - Active Listening

Active listening – a concept we have all heard before, but how often do we consciously practice it? As a leader, your ability to actively listen can make a **world** of difference in your team's productivity, morale, and overall performance.

Active listening is the act of completely focusing on the message that someone, in this example your team member, is trying to express and reacting in a manner that displays that you have heard and understood their message. Too often we listen just enough to prepare an immediate reply. True active listening requires paying attention to the words being stated, the speaker's tone of voice, their body language, and their emotions.

When is active listening needed? The simple answer is always! People deserve to be heard. In business, active listening is especially important in any conversation where comprehension and effective communication are key. Whether delivering feedback to a team member, settling a problem, or just chatting, active listening can help you establish stronger connections and accomplish better results.

So how can you increase your active listening skills? Here are the five strategies:

1. Be Present

Give the speaker your full attention by consciously tuning in, removing distractions, and concentrating on the dialogue.

2. Ask Questions

Clarify any confusing points or seek extra information to show that you are involved and interested.

3. Paraphrase

Summarize or repeat what the speaker said in your own words to confirm that you have understood their points properly.

4. Reflect

Take time to think through what they have stated before responding. Exhibit empathy by recognizing the speaker's experiences and emotions.

5. Avoid interrupting

Allow the speaker to complete their thoughts before reacting and avoid stepping in with your ideas or views.

Active listening may be one of the most undervalued qualities in leadership, yet it can make all the difference. By adopting these tactics into your everyday discussions, you become a better listener and a more successful leader. It does take practice and being conscious in your interactions. Learning the skill is worth it. Your team members will feel truly heard and appreciated, leading to improved trust and cooperation.

Skill #2 - Verbal and Non-Verbal Cues

Picture this: You're on video conferencing call with your team discussing the latest project developments. You observe that one of your team members looks disengaged, slouching in their chair and avoiding eye contact with the screen. You recognize this might indicate apathy or disagreement with the project's direction, or disinterest in their part of the work product. But how can you understand these non-verbal clues and address them appropriately?

Accurately assessing verbal and non-verbal communication are equally useful weapons in every leader's armory. Verbal communication incorporates not only the words we use, but the tone of voice and the ultimate clarity of our message. Non-verbal communication, on the other hand, relates to our body language, facial expressions, and other physical indicators that may transmit meaning without words.

As a facilitative leader, it is necessary to grasp both types of communication, process them accurately, and react to them appropriately. The following are ways to enhance your verbal and non-verbal communication skills.

Verbal Communication

Be Clear: When communicating with your team, be straightforward and concise. Avoid using technical jargon or complex terminology that might confuse your team members. Simple direct communication also minimizes interpretation errors.

Listen Actively: Listening is a fundamental element of verbal communication. Be sure you consciously focus on your team members when they are speaking, fully absorbing their message, and responding properly.

Use Positive Language: Positive edifying words, even when addressing a negative situation, can encourage and inspire your team members. Concentrate on choosing words that communicate support, helpfulness, and praise rather than pettiness and condemnation.

Non-Verbal Communication

Pay Attention: Non-verbal signs might be subtle, so consciously paying attention to your team members' body language and facial expressions when they are communicating is critical. Inconsistencies between the words they are using, tone, and unconscious facial cues may identify red flags that may need to be addressed.

Keep Eye Contact: Eye contact is a strong non-verbal sign that expresses confidence, attention, and respect. It is wise to keep eye contact while interacting with your team members.

Be Aware of Your Own Body Language: Your body language may also communicate messages. Sit up straight, keep your chin up, smile, hold an open stance, and avoid crossing your arms or knees, which might suggest defensiveness.

Ultimately, leading with empathy in a remote work setting thrives with a mix of advanced communication skills, emotional integrity, and a dedication to fostering a supportive and collaborative workplace. Emotional intelligence is a leadership skill that can improve connection and empathetic interactions, making our team stronger and more cohesive. Before we dive into emotional intelligence in the next chapter, take a moment to reflect on the areas you might improve your communication skills:

1. Do I choose to actively listen to my employees, or do I multi-task while they are speaking?

_____

_____

_____

_____

2. Do I notice team members' body language during meetings?

_____

_____

_____

_____

3. Am I offering clear language when I speak, or do I sometimes ramble, getting off the subject, creating confusion for the team?

_____

_____

_____

_____

Chapter 4 Developing Emotional Intelligence

As leaders and managers, we often focus on our intellectual intelligence - after all, it is what got us promoted into our positions in the first place, right? But what about <u>emotional</u> intelligence? Do we understand the importance of it in the successful leadership of our teams?

Think about it: how often have you been in a meeting where someone's feelings interfered with a useful discussion? Alternatively, maybe you acted in error because you misinterpreted a coworker's emotional state. We can manage these circumstances more skillfully by developing our emotional intelligence. This chapter examines emotional intelligence, its significance, and how practicing it can help us, and our teams, as we continue our quest to become emotionally intelligent leaders.

Understanding Emotional Intelligence

The ability to comprehend, control, and react to our own emotions and the emotions of others is known as emotional intelligence. It entails consciousness of your own emotions and being able to connect and sympathize with people around you. But why is it crucial in a professional situation to have emotional intelligence? Because it just might result in improved teamwork and communication. A more open and effective work atmosphere can result from relating to and understanding your coworkers on an emotional level.

Also, emotional awareness can aid your ability to manage challenging situations with delicacy and poise. Having a high level of emotional recognition can assist you in remaining calm and focused while dealing with difficult people or negotiating difficult circumstances, leading to better decisions and win-win outcomes.

Leaders Can Develop Emotional Intelligence

The elusive attribute that distinguishes outstanding leaders from the rest is the genuine application of emotional intelligence. It involves reading a room, comprehending other people's emotions, and reacting in a way that brings out the best in everyone. Is this ability a natural trait or one you can learn?

A CEO named Emily was known for her direct and unemotional management style. She was results-oriented and had little time for feelings. She thought that emotions were a distraction from the task at hand and that her team ought to be able to overcome difficulties without becoming embroiled in emotions.

Emily presided over a meeting with her executive team. Tensions were at an all-time high as they discussed a new product launch that had encountered difficulties. One of Emily's team members, Jane, grew more and more upset as the discussion heated up. When she began to weep, Emily quickly stopped her. She yelled, "We don't have time for this. Rather than wallow in self-pity and frustration, we must concentrate on finding a solution."

The team eventually did find a solution to the issue as the meeting proceeded. Afterward, Emily became aware that she did not handle Jane's weeping situation appropriately and had entirely disregarded the feelings of her team members since she had been so intent on the result. She felt uneasy for not realizing at the time that her leadership style had made Jane feel unsupported and unappreciated.

Not sure what to do, Emily stumbled across the term emotional intelligence. She began to research it, studied books, attended courses, and even engaged a coach to hone her ability. She discovered that feelings are an integral component of any activity rather than a distraction from it. She was missing important information and preventing her staff from giving their best effort by ignoring their emotions.

Emily began practicing methods for developing personal emotional intelligence. She increased her self-awareness, engaged in active listening, and began observing body language. She learned to display more empathy and provided and accepted constructive criticism.

Emily saw a meaningful change in her team's culture over time. Communication became more open and honest as people began to feel more at ease expressing their opinions and emotions. The team started to perform better due to the increased sense of trust and cooperation. And Emily's emotional intelligence evolution was the catalyst of the improved culture.

As we continue through this chapter, you will come to understand the significance of this learned behavior.

The Four Components of Emotional Intelligence

Imagine being a leader who can sense the moods of your team members, adjust to them, and use them to propel the team toward success. It's not magic, it is emotional intelligence. Emotional awareness of yourself and your team members is another pillar of outstanding leadership. It consists of four components:

- Self-awareness
- Self-management
- Social awareness
- Relationship management

These four elements are intertwined and can help a manager understand and connect with the team on a deeper level.

Self-awareness is the foundation of emotional intelligence. As a leader, you must <u>understand</u> <u>your</u> <u>emotions</u>, strengths, weaknesses, and biases. This awareness helps you make better decisions, respond appropriately to situations, and maintain a level head under pressure.

Self-management is the ability to <u>control</u> <u>your emotions</u>, thoughts, and actions. A leader who can manage their emotions can inspire their team, remain calm under tension, and set a positive example for others. Personal emotional management powers better decisions, manages your time effectively, and handles conflicts gracefully.

Social awareness is the ability to <u>understand another's</u> <u>emotions</u> and needs. It allows you to "read" body language, notice social cues, and sense a room's energy or mood.

Relationship management is building one-on-one connections with others. Communicating effectively, leading by example, and inspiring others contributes to strong relationships. As a leader, you must connect with your team on a personal level, motivate them, and create a culture of trust and respect. Effective successful leadership is dependent on emotional intelligence.

Practical Tips and Techniques for Building Emotional Intelligence

You can choose to improve your emotional awareness of yourself and others by integrating several useful strategies:

--Make an effort to use active listening skills

Paying close attention to another person's message, without interjecting, being distracted, or preparing a response, can open your mind to receiving more information that you may have missed in previous communications. Contrary to what Emily did when she interrupted and spoke harshly to Jane, try to understand their viewpoint and validate their emotions.

--Pay attention to how YOU are acting

It is crucial to be aware of the signals we may be conveying with posture, facial expressions, and tone of voice. Our attitude can influence the context of the message as it is being communicated.

--Develop self-awareness

You must be open to feeling your own emotions to comprehend those of others. Spend time considering your feelings and your emotional responses in high trigger situations and strive to direct them in a positive way.

--Demonstrate empathy

Do your best to step into another person's situation and attempt to understand their perspective. Even if you do not agree, try to assimilate their viewpoint and respond in a way that respects their feelings. Emily was able to recognize her deficiency in this area only after she had replied abruptly to her teammates. Although the answer came too late, she will have the foresight for future interactions.

Like Emily eventually did, you can improve your emotional intelligence and become a more effective leader by adopting these methods into your leadership style. Remember that practicing the four elements of emotional intelligence and being willing to grow is more important than being perfect in every situation.

Let's now step back and consider the underlying meaning of Emily's story. Although Emily was a gifted leader, she lacked one important quality: emotional intelligence. She mistakenly believed that being tough and results-oriented was all it took to motivate a team to make things happen. She discovered there was more to it. Building a culture of trust and cooperation requires recognizing and responding to human emotions.

1. What is my emotional intelligence quotient? Of the 4 components, where can I improve?

_____

_____

_____

_____

2. What specific tips could be useful to leverage emotional awareness within my team?

_____

_____

_____

_____

3. Are there organizational coaching or training resources that can help?

_____

_____

_____

Chapter 5 Fostering Empathy in Teams

Leaders have the enormous challenge of motivating our teams to function as smoothly as a well-oiled machine. Creating a cohesive team that produces results in a remote work setting increases the complexity of this task. When team members are physically separated, they can lack the sense of community and collaboration that comes with sharing a workspace.

How, then, can we close the empathy gap within our teams? Despite our separation, how can we foster a sense of camaraderie, belonging, and mutual respect? In this chapter, we will examine various methods and approaches that can assist you in achieving this goal. Team-building exercise examples and ideas to establish a welcoming workplace are shared. Even the elusive skill of inspiring cooperation is covered since, let's face it, sometimes managing workers feels like herding cats!

Have fun with team-building exercises...

Team-building exercises are one way to bring teammates together, foster close relationships, and have some fun! Activities that promote empathy and a sense of community when people are not physically together can cause a manager to pause. What types of exercises would be most effective? Below are some proven team-building ideas to try out whether in-person or on a video conference call.

There are many types of traditional icebreaker activities that can be used in a virtual setting. Begin a team meeting with a round of individual check-ins and invite each team member to share something personal, such as a bucket list experience, a highlight of their week so far, a show and tell item, or even a baby picture! You can even create short games, such as brainstorming words starting with a chosen alphabet letter for a specific category, or a few trivia questions. There are many online resources to fuel your ideas. Encouraging engagement, sharing, and a little laughter is the goal. It may sound corny, but it works!

Next, try a virtual scavenger hunt. After dividing team members into pairs, give them a list of items they must locate at their separate worksites. Items as simple as a book with a blue cover or a coffee mug with a clever slogan are good examples. This exercise promotes teamwork, problem-solving, and a little constructive competitiveness.

A virtual book club is yet another great idea for team building. Pick a book related to your team's interest or industry, then schedule a virtual chapter discussion once per week for example. This activity promotes both individual and team growth and offers a forum for candid discussions about the concepts of the book and how they may apply to the organization's objectives.

Remember that empathy is about connecting with and understanding others. These exercises may be incorporated into your remote work routine to help your team become more cohesive and to lay a foundation of the importance of connectedness. So have fun, be inventive, and observe how these types of activities can help strengthen the bonds of your team.

Establish a welcoming and safe atmosphere...

A secure and accepting atmosphere is vital to an employee's impression of a positive work culture. It creates a sense of safety and encourages staff members to express themselves authentically. It provides the context in which team members communicate and connect, even within the framework of a remote work environment.

First, establishing a basis of trust and confidence among team members is necessary. Regular check-ins, team-building exercises, and transparent communication contribute to building these ideals. Actively facilitate a protective setting for team members to express themselves without worrying about criticism or retaliation. Establish impartial guidelines that set the stage for respectful communication among every person.

Next, work to foster an inclusive culture. Ensure everyone feels valued and respected, regardless of their origin, gender, ethnicity, or any other characteristics. Promote diversity and allow team members to contribute their distinctive viewpoints and experiences.

Encourage team members to acknowledge each other and show respect. Active listening and sincerely making an effort to comprehend others' viewpoints can impact a team's cohesiveness. As the leader, affirm their thoughts and feelings while showing your concern for their wellbeing.

Additionally, offer opportunities to stimulate collaboration and teamwork. Team members are more likely to grow in empathy for one another when they work together to achieve a common goal. To create a cohesive working environment, promote cross-functional projects, brainstorming sessions, and peer feedback.

Lastly, set an example. Model empathy for your team by demonstrating what it looks like. Show that you care about each team member individually by being receptive to comments, willing to listen, and open to suggestions.

Although it may take time to evolve, a secure and welcoming environment for remote workers is essential for creating a powerful team. By choosing to make a collective culture a priority, a leader or manager can establish a virtual workplace where empathy flourishes and team members feel encouraged, respected, and heard.

Promoting cooperation is key...

You may be thinking, "Collaboration is a given. Our team <u>must</u> cooperate to meet the company's objectives!" Teamwork is more than merely crossing items off a to-do list and meeting deadlines. Enabling cooperation nurtures a sense of belonging and connection throughout your remote workforce. By giving team members a chance to communicate ideas, viewpoints, and experiences with one another, trust inevitably grows.

As we have learned throughout this dialogue, empathy and trust go hand in hand. Team members are more likely to be open and vulnerable when they trust one another. And they are more receptive to hearing and assimilating one another's viewpoints. Also, they are more inclined to stand up for one another and stand by one another when circumstances take a turn for the worse.

Utilizing technological tools can improve collaboration and create efficiencies in the process, especially when the team is segregated. There are innovative software packages that track assignments, schedule team meetings, assign project duties, and share documents as part of project management. Resource references are noted at the back of this book.

How do you cultivate attitudes of cooperation among your remote team members? Some of the previous ideas discussed also play a part here:

- *Plan regular team check-ins and meetings*
- *Create a workspace where staff feel encouraged to communicate their thoughts and opinions*
- *Advocate for an inclusive culture*
- *Use technology applications for efficient project management*

As the team leader, it is your job to be a facilitator to connect the team members, to initiate the evolution of an open and secure workplace, and to promote opportunities for cooperation. Safe and supported workers create a strong cohesive team, which performs better to ultimately meet the organization's highest objectives.

1. Have I used team-building exercises in the past, which ones, and what was the outcome?

   _____

   _____

   _____

   _____

2. Take a deeper dive into the organization's, and the team's, culture. Is there a spirit of cooperation, or dissention in the ranks? Do the members speak up, or shut down?

   _____

   _____

   _____

   _____

3. Candidly assess the strengths and weaknesses of the team's dynamics, communication, and peer-to-peer interaction.

   _____

   _____

   _____

   _____

Chapter 6 Overcoming Challenges

All leaders will face challenges. And you are expected to resolve them with grace and resilience, whether it is a project gone wrong, a team member performing below expectations, or a painful conversation that needs to be held.

So, what is the best way to handle these difficulties, especially when they show up in a remote working setting? We'll look at some methods and approaches in this chapter that can assist in managing challenging circumstances and maintaining empathy. All managers and leaders must develop the skills to settle conflicts, initiate uncomfortable conversations, and maintain poise and fairness in trying circumstances. Examples demonstrating the value of these abilities and the tools needed to deal with these situations successfully are shared below.

Managing Conflict

At one point in my career, I managed a team that included two individuals often at odds with one another. They were almost entirely dissimilar in personalities, working methods, and task-approaches. They would often disagree with each other in loud voices in meetings, affecting not only the overall team's output but also its morale.

To address the disruptive nature of their interactions, I first planned a private meeting with each team member to better understand their viewpoints before attempting to resolve the problem. I then called a meeting with both members, directing open dialogue and encouraging attentive listening. I clarified that while some conflict was normal and good, it needed to be handled positively and with respect for each other and for the team.

We created a specific strategy that these two members could employ when disagreements arose in the future. We were able to find the common ground that they did share and restored confidence through recognizing and accepting each of their perspectives. Although conflict will inevitably arise, it can be properly managed to build a stronger, more unified team.

Tools: Active listening, individual and group discussions, root cause analysis, and communication plan development.

Handling Contentious Discussions

On another occasion, a colleague needed some advice about a difficult meeting with a team member who was constantly performing below par. The chat was expected to be difficult because the subject often became emotional when addressed with any type of criticism.

I encouraged my colleague to prepare by collecting the information and facts necessary to support the constructive criticism. Also, taking the time to recognize and step into the shoes of the team member and how he or she may respond to the dialogue can be helpful in deciding the tone and phrasing of the message. The colleague shared with me after the conversation that he consciously chose to be empathetic and compassionate throughout the talk, expressing to the team member his wish of their

71

success and providing assistance and tools to help them advance.

Despite the tense discussion, the employee appreciated the honesty and readiness to help. A strategy to address the performance concerns was agreed upon, and, within days, dramatic improvement occurred. Even though uncomfortable conversations are not fun, they must happen, and the manager must often lead them. With preparation, setting the goal for the discussion, and employing empathy, these contentious conversations can produce fruitful results.

Tools: Planning, collection of information and facts, tapping resources and support, active listening, a clear path to an intended outcome, and a compassionate approach.

Maintaining Composure During Trying Circumstances

I previously worked with a teammate, Mark, who was having some personal problems at home which were affecting his job performance. He was consistently late in his attendance and could not concentrate on tasks for more than short periods of time. Mark would often fail to meet deadlines, which caused delays with other team members who were relying on him.

Once this issue was brought to my attention, I began to check in with Mark often, helping him with time management scheduling, encouraging him to reach out to the employee assistance program of the human resources office, and offering personal support. I also assured the other team members that Mark's work product would be presented on time, so that their tasks could be completed by their respective deadlines. An experience such as this one exemplifies that displaying empathy in everyday conversations and providing support in difficult circumstances can have a positive impact.

Tools: Frequent individual check-ins, knowledge of employee assistance program resources, time management plan development, team communication, and a caring attitude.

Handling conflicts between staff members, navigating an uncomfortable conversation with an individual, and displaying empathy in trying circumstances are essential skills for any manager or leader. Offering resources and support, active listening, and clear planning are critical components to effective resolution of these types of situations. Leading with empathy supports teams through difficult challenges and develops stronger ties.

By now you are recognizing the value of empathy in the workplace. Empathetic leadership can transform a work culture and build loyalty within your team. It does take time to solidify such a culture, especially in a remote work team. And once you have built it, how do you preserve it?

1. How do I handle conflict or maintain composure in tough situations?

_____

_____

_____

_____

2. How does the team react when under pressure or in difficult circumstances?

_____

_____

_____

_____

Chapter 7 Sustaining Empathy Within A Remote Team

Fostering an empathetic working atmosphere is like nurturing a plant. Even if you carefully plant and water the seeds and allow the seedlings to take root and grow, mature plants will not continue to flourish unless you provide ongoing care. Similarly, an uplifting organizational culture needs continual care and work to maintain its strength.

A manager named Amy became all too aware of this. She had assembled a group of people who liked each other and had the ability to work together efficiently. The coworkers got along well and helped each other without being asked. Yet Amy noticed that as the team grew larger in number, it was becoming more difficult to maintain these personal connections.

She overheard a dispute between two team members. She decided to take a back seat and observe rather than intervene and mediate immediately. She realized that the issue was not a problem with the task but a miscommunication between the two due to a difference in communication styles. Amy had an idea. She asked that each member share their preferred method of communication during a team meeting. They each shared how they liked to receive feedback, how they preferred to communicate, and how they handled conflict.

Amy then required everyone to attend a training class on interpersonal communication. The training was helpful and constructive, and, through it, the team members were better able to recognize others' communication styles and adapt to them.

Amy recognized that maintaining empathy within the team culture requires consistent effort, flexibility, and a readiness to listen and learn. She supported personal development and evaluated success in terms of not only the tasks completed but the quality of the bonds formed within the team itself.

As a leader, you can help your team maintain empathy in their interactions by observing and becoming aware of both individual and team needs, promoting open communication, and supporting feedback and improvement. Empathy and respect will continue to grow and blossom, much like a well-kept garden, making the workplace happy and productive.

Long-term Empathy Maintenance

A leader must learn to display empathy and allow the team members to see it in action regularly. Developing a habit of consistent empathy in your interactions with your remote team will set the expectation and the example for others to follow.

First, you must truly listen to and assimilate what your team members are saying. They are trying to send you, and others, a message. Ensure that they have your full attention even when you are not in the same room. Also, show your concern by routinely checking in with each member individually and inquiring about their personal and professional progress. Do your best to grasp their perspective and put yourself in their position. Ask questions to better understand their message. And lastly, show genuine empathy. Do not just act the part, show your team members that you sincerely care about them and their wellbeing.

Encouraging Development and Growth

It is your duty as a leader to support the personal and professional development of your team members. When each team member grows and improves their skills, it benefits the whole team. Yet, to actively build a culture of continual development, an open environment of constructive feedback is necessary.

One method to perpetuate this type of culture is soliciting team members' opinions and ideas. What aspect of their profession do they find enjoyable? What difficulties do they encounter? How can you as a leader help them more effectively? You can learn a lot by posing these questions and receiving your team members' comments. Implementing changes based on their ideas and thoughts will also make them feel heard and valued in the organization.

Offering opportunities for education and advancement clearly promotes individual development. Extending to your team members paid training classes, mentorship programs, or special projects that appeal to their passions and interests can motivate them to develop their skills and talents to the benefit of the organization. Some companies even offer financial assistance to pursue a higher education degree or a specialized designation or certification.

In the end, it is important to keep in mind that development and growth are continuing processes. As a leader, you must be dedicated to fostering a culture where learning and professional growth are valued and encouraged if you want to support the development of your team.

Validating Success

Judging progress of an empathetic culture in a remote work setting is not a quantitative measurement, but a qualitative one. After all, empathy, compassion, and team building are characteristics that may be difficult to measure in numbers or dollars. Yet, there are significant signs that can identify if your team is headed in the correct direction. One important indicator is that your team members feel at ease approaching you not only with successes and positive developments, but also with issues and problems. By doing so, they are acknowledging their trust in you, believing that you will respond in a supportive and helpful manner. Also, it is a clear sign that you are cultivating a healthy work atmosphere if you notice an improvement in productivity, engagement, and morale among your team members.

When a leader has worked hard to establish a climate of mutual understanding and support, it is rewarding to see the tangible results and productivity of such a work environment. When team members feel motivated to do their best and continue to expand their personal and professional horizons, these are indicators of a well-balanced and healthy team. A leader's positive impact on their staff members' work life is ultimately the most significant indicator of leadership performance.

1. Am I actively setting a positive example for the team?

_____

_____

_____

_____

2. Do I ask for, and am I open to, my team members' opinions and thoughts about the organization, the projects, the work processes, etc.?

_____

_____

_____

_____

3. Are opportunities for professional growth and promotion supported within the organization?

_____

_____

_____

_____

Conclusion

The world of remote work poses challenges all its own. It has become essential to consciously employ empathy in this new environment. As a leader or manager, you can empower your team by fostering a culture of empathy that encourages communication, inclusivity, and collaboration. You can develop your skills to become the manager who overcomes any obstacle by learning the science behind empathy and realizing its advantages in leadership.

The ideals of active listening, effective communication, emotional intelligence, and team building advance a welcoming environment necessary to promote empathy in a remote work context. Building an empathetic culture also calls for a readiness to go beyond your own perspective and consider the perspective of others - walking a mile in their shoes. By applying the strategies and examples shared throughout this book, you can establish a work environment that is both rewarding and productive.

Maintaining a positive work atmosphere also depends on how well conflict and uncomfortable topics are managed. You can ease tension, build mutual respect among your team members, and defuse conflict by treating these circumstances with empathy and understanding. Sustaining an empathetic culture requires dedication to improvement through observation, feedback, and assessment of interactions within the team.

Empathy-based leadership is key to effective management and productivity in a remote work environment. A workplace, remote or otherwise, where each member has a level of trust, feels connection with the team, works efficiently, and contributes to the organization's bottom line is ultimately the goal.

So, ask yourself, how can I better include empathy in my leadership style? With the knowledge gained through this discussion, consider your own experiences in the workplace. How have you handled difficult situations in the past? How might you handle them differently in the future? We all have the ability to grow, change, and develop into compassionate leaders.

Additionally, creating a culture of empathy and connection within your team or organization is a worthy goal. An empathetic culture promotes dynamic communication, team synergy, and elevated productivity. What are some ideas that you can implement immediately with your remote work staff to begin the process of developing a healthy team environment? It is worth the effort.

Additional Notes/Thoughts/To Do Items:

References and More Information

Introduction and Chapter 1

1. Definitions of empathy: https://www.merriam-webster.com/dictionary/empathy; https://dictionary.cambridge.org/dictionary/english/empathy https://dictionary.apa.org/empathy

2. Neuronal resonance: https://www.biorxiv.org/content/10.1101/2020.05.26.117309v1.full

3. Emotional regulation: https://www.betterup.com/blog/emotional-regulation-skills

4. Active listening: https://www.verywellmind.com/what-is-active-listening-3024343

5. Perspective-taking: https://knowledge.wharton.upenn.edu/article/perspective-taking-brain-hack-can-help-make-better-decisions/

6. Emotional management: https://www.indeed.com/career-advice/career-development/emotional-management-skills

Chapter 2

7. Remote work challenges: https://www.indeed.com/career-advice/career-development/working-remotely

Chapter 3

8. Active Listening: https://www.coursera.org/articles/active-listening

9. Verbal and Non-Verbal Communication: https://www.marketingweek.com/lorraine-heggessey-praise-leader/

Chapter 4

10. Intellectual Intelligence: https://www.igi-global.com/dictionary/launching-diversity-intelligent-strategies-in-organizations/87885

11. Emotional Intelligence Components: https://www.medicalnewstoday.com/articles/components-of-emotional-intelligence

12. Emotional Awareness: https://www.ncbi.nlm.nih.gov/pmc/articles/PMC8395748/

Chapter 5

13. Ice-Breaker Exercises: https://blog.hubspot.com/marketing/ice-breaker-games

14. Virtual Scavenger Hunts: Virtual Scavenger Hunt Ideas & Sample Lists (teambuilding.com)

15. The Empathy-Trust Connection: https://www.weeve.ai/post/empathy-is-the-foundation-of-trust

16. Assessing Technology: https://www.techtarget.com/searchhrsoftware/featur

e/Hybrid-workplace-technologies-to-power-future-of-work

17. Collaboration Tools: https://resources.workable.com/tutorial/collaboration-tools

Chapter 6

18. Workplace Obstacles: https://ca.indeed.com/career-advice/career-development/workplace-challenges

Chapter 7

19. Culture Sustainability: https://www.forbes.com/sites/tracybrower/2021/02/07/how-to-sustain-company-culture-in-a-hybrid-work-model/?sh=6f385f091009

Additional Information Resources

20. https://adevait.com/blog/remote-work/empathy-in-the-remote-world

21. https://cloudemployee.co.uk/blog/mindset-growth/empathy-is-the-key-to-leadership-in-a-remote-setting

22. https://www.forbes.com/sites/forbescoachescouncil/2020/10/12/14-authentic-ways-to-demonstrate-empathy-when-leading-remotely/?sh=266adc97467d

23. https://www.businessolver.com/workplace-empathy

24. https://www.athyna.io/blog-posts/how-leaders-should-use-empathy-to-energize-remote-teams-for-success

25. https://hbr.org/2020/07/remote-managers-are-having-trust-issues

About The Author

Melissa Harris is a CEO-Director of a large public entity risk management organization, where she has established a culture of leading-edge innovation with uncompromising integrity, and mentored team members to greater heights in their abilities and personal fulfillment in their contributions. She has spent the last several years refining organizational leadership, developing high performing staff, and promoting exceptional customer service for clients. She is also an experienced public speaker, actress, and business entrepreneur. Her passions include researching and writing about personal development in the areas of business, leadership, life balance, and spirituality. She believes everyone is born with a purpose and we are called to inspire each other to embrace our gifts and share them with the world.

About The Publisher

The mission of Vue Claire is to promote, publish, and market written, video and audio works that encourage personal and professional development in the areas of business, leadership, life balance, and spirituality.

www.ingramcontent.com/pod-product-compliance
Lightning Source LLC
Chambersburg PA
CBHW070026030426
42335CB00017B/2316